To Str... 'p

Soulmates

JOURNAL

Soulmates
JOURNAL

by

J. A. HUSS

Find me at
Jahuss.com

Cover design by J. A. Huss
Copyright © 2015 by J. A. Huss
Interior Designed and Formatted by Tianne Samson
with E.M. Tippetts Book Designs
emtippettsbookdesigns.com

ISBN- 978-1-936413-84-3

Books by
J.A. Huss

Dedication

For Jana.

This was all her idea and she worked hard to pull it together.
Thank you so much for all that you do.

XXOO♥♥✿

Tragic

"I'll do what I want. And staying away from her isn't even in
the top million things I want to do with that girl."

"I will say with one hundred percent certainty
that you will come tonight."
-Tragic

_____

_____
_____

_____

_____

_____

_____

_____

_____

_____

_____

_____

_____

_____

_____

_____

_____

_____

_____

If I wanted to change my life then I'd have to do it myself. Because no one was coming.
-Tragic

"Sweetheart, you won't get far here if we can't touch you."
-Tragic

Ronin takes my hand and leads me out to the terrace and when I step over that threshold I feel it in my bones. Nothing in my life will ever be the same after this.
-Tragic

"Ronin Flynn, you might undo me."
-Tragic

"I think you overestimate me, Ronin. It wasn't courage,
it was desperation and fear."
-Tragic

No matter how freaking nice that rug is under your feet, someone always pulls it out from under you eventually.
-Tragic

"But no matter what happens - you will never shrink back into a corner from me again. Because I will never hurt you."
-Tragic

He's one cute guy and all. But he's not for me. Even if he is tall and has those amazing blue eyes. I bet if we had babies our kids would totally have the most cornflower blue eyes ever. And dark raven hair. Oh God, we'd make little model babies. They'd need agents at birth.

-Tragic

Manic

"I want kissing, I want mad fucking passionate kissing. The kind of kissing I've seen in all those other photos of you, the kissing that is so filled with emotion and longing and lust, I'm instantly hard. Kiss me like that, Blackbird."

"I'm not running away. I never look back, I only move forward."
-Manic

"I'm not a runner. I'm a slow walker at best, possibly a shuffler, or an aimless wanderer, but never a runner."
-Manic

It's just me, Ronin and this asshole named after a truck.
-Manic

"So, tell me, Ford- is that a family name? Or did
your parents just like trucks?"
-Manic

"If she can be stolen, then she was never yours to begin with."
-Manic

The journey is the only thing that counts because once you reach your destination there's always somewhere else to go.
-Manic

'Wow, Ford, you're a total asshole, arent' you?"
-Manic

The secret to the perfect job is to keep it
easy. Very predictable.
-Manic

"Are you sure you want the real reason? Because most people prefer white lies to truth."
-Manic

Panic

"You are my forever guy. I'd just like to say that right now.
You are my forever guy."

"That's my dirtiest secret and now you have it. I just don't give a fuck about people, I really don't."
-Panic

"I like you. I'd like to show you how much, actually. I'm being a gentleman to make life easier for you, but believe me, it's not really in my nature to be so accommodating. I typically just take what I want."
-Panic

"It changes nothing for me, because the difference between you and Ronin is that you're looking for the girl I was and he's looking for the girl I want to be."
-Panic

"I'm seething with jealousy. It infuriates me that time and time again he gets what he wants. Ronin pulls love towards him like he's gravity." I stop to laugh. "He only has to ask and love appears in his life. And me? I beg for it. I want love more than anything, yet everyone thinks I'm insufferable."
-Panic

I'm just one single tragic girl, what can I do?
-Panic

You need to experience all that fear and pain
and desperation. You need to see all that stuff
because at the end of all those bad things there
is a sweet and gentle man named Ronin Flynn.
-Panic

"I want to marry you. Like yesterday. But I know that's not gonna happen just yet, so I just want you to know, I can wait."
-Panic

"Rook, I'm not a risk, I'm a sure thing."
-Panic

"If you touch me I'll touch you back. I'll cup your face and kiss your mouth. I'll hold you close and make you choose me."
-Panic

"I'd never walk out, I'd fight for you every single time. You'd never have to wonder if I'd be there because I'd show the fuck up before that thought could ever cross your mind."
-Panic

She makes my heart ache. Literally. My chest feels like it's gonna be ripped apart from the longing, that's how much I love this girl.
-Panic

Ronin might not be perfect, but he's close enough for me. I want him, I love him, and he's mine.
-Panic

SLACK

Once again I ask myself why? Why the fuck do these bitches put up with me?

To Ford's friend who is a girl. He likes you a lot, but I'm gonna try and steal his heart when I get my braces off, so you better move fast.
-Slack

He's lucky that loyalty is my number one moral value. Maybe my only moral value. I do, after all, steal, cheat, lie, and lust.
-Slack

I'm a freak looking for a freak. A freak that can relate to me.
-Slack

"I don't want you to leave, Ford. I'm not sure life without you is possible."
-Slack

"Why the fuck would you ever agree to my conditions? Why?"
-Slack

"I'm gonna fuck that banker, Ford. The minute he asks, because my goddamned vibrator is broken and the fucking mall sold out of the fucking Hitachi model I like, and won't be getting anymore in until after fucking New Year's!"
-Slack

Holy shit. Veronica is intense.
-Slack

"You're a good pet."
-Slack

"I don't like the gagging, pet."
-Slack

She takes the punishments, she likes it in the
ass, and she comes for me on command.
-Slack

I am the first to admit that my rules are unreasonable. My behavior is atrocious. My indifference is derogatory.
-Slack

Rook is friendly, so maybe she likes friendly guys?
Ronin is friendly. And Spencer even more so. So I
figure if I want Rook to like me, then I should try to
emulate the other people in her life whom she likes.
-Slack

I like Ronin these days, he's not a bad guy. But why does he always get the fucking girl?
-Slack

Holy shit that almost cracks my black Grinch heart.
-Slack

"You should look for something for your friend who is a girl."
-Slack

_____
_____
_____
_____
_____
_____
_____
_____
_____
_____
_____
_____
_____
_____
_____
_____
_____
_____
_____
_____
_____
_____

"Come with me. I'll let you snoop though all his stuff."
-Slack

"Fuck you, Ford."
-Slack

_____
_____
_____
_____
_____
_____
_____
_____
_____
_____
_____
_____
_____
_____
_____
_____
_____
_____
_____
_____
_____

"You can talk if you stay, but I'm not going to pretend I like you for your witty conversation. I like you for your pussy and I'd like to fuck you tonight. I'm tired of playing. Stay and have fun or get the hell out."
-Slack

I'm not capable of much empathy, but I can fake it. And they never know the difference, so what the fuck. It doesn't cost me anything to pretend to understand and be nice.
-Slack

TAUT

"You're like crazy sexy, Ford. And all this weird shit you do, that just adds to it. I'm not sure why, but I like your strangeness. It's real and it drives me a little wild."

I have a thing for throats. Maybe some guys like tits and pussy. I like tits and pussy. But throats. Fuck. That shit turns me on.
-Taut

I'm sure this is what ticked me off as a baby. The fact
that they were constantly touching me. I suspect
it's the reason I refused to talk to them.
-Taut

"I want to be won, Ford. If you can win me, you can have me. I'll be yours and you'll have earned it."
-Taut

It's just... what the fuck? Why? It's like I have a sign
on my fucking head that says I like the weird ones.
-Taut

"So you think I'm a hot serial killer? And you're still here because... it's okay to be a serial killer as long as I'm eye-candy?"
-Taut

I let Ronin keep Rook, but Ashleigh is mine. And I'm
not giving her up without a fight.
-Taut

"What do you like, Ashleigh? You like it slow and tender? Because if so, you're out of luck. I'm not that kind of guy."
-Taut

"I can pull you taut, Ashleigh. Like the poems. I
can bring you back together."
-Taut

I spy Rook standing just inside the door with Veronica. They are thick as thieves these days. If I were Spencer I'd watch out. They will be in trouble soon, if they're not already.
-Taut

When I was a kid I knew I was a genius. No one had to tell me, and maybe that sounds... what? Egotistical? Conceited? Boastful? Arrogant? Prideful? And if I extrapolate out a little bit, it probably borders on selfish and indifferent as well. But it is what it is. I'm fucking smart. Im beyond fucking smart. I'm an intellectual anomaly.

-Taut

"That's a hard lesson to learn. You should never save anything for something special."
-Taut

"Believe me, I'm not into hurting girls. I'd rather make you squeal my name in pleasure."
-Taut

I wanted to be invested in it and I didn't want it to be perfect. I wanted it to be flawed. I wanted it to be a work in progress. I wanted to rescue it.
-Taut

"I'm in Ashleigh. I want you, I want Kate, I want this.
I want to sleep with you every night and give
you everything you want. I'm in."
-Taut

"Sphere of privacy, people. Now."
-Taut

"He was always doing that sphere stuff when we were kids. Keep out of my sphere, back off my sphere. No one was allowed in his sphere."
-Taut

"You're so stupid, Ford."
-Taut

"Ford, the promise of your full sexual attention is just
about the highlight of my life right now, why pretend?"
-Taut

I'd like to be half of something. I'd like that
emptiness to go away.
-Taut

_____

_____

_____

_____

_____

_____

_____

_____

_____

_____

_____

_____

_____

_____

_____

_____

_____

_____

BOMB

But I'm a businessman too. I might not look like one,
but I am all fucking business.

I stalked her good. I'm an accomplished stalker.
-Bomb

I own her ass.
-Bomb

"I think you just changed my life Spencer Shrike."
"That was the plan, Bombshell. That was always the plan."
-Bomb

"Do you like the dirty talk, Bombshell? Does it turn you on?"
-Bomb

"If you're here to fuck me tonight, the answer
is no. I have a boyfriend."
-Bomb

"They're not really dogs, they're employees. Security. I paid forty grand a piece for these fucking dogs. One wrong look at Ashleigh or Kate and they eat your face off."
-Bomb

Ronnie is mine. Ronnie has always been mine.
-Bomb

I can almost hear her heartbeat, that wild heartbeat
that drives me crazy beating against mine as she
lies on top of me after sex.
-Bomb

My name is the shit. Spencer Shrike.
-Bomb

My Shrike Sense is tingling.
-Bomb

GUNS

"Veronica," he whispers. "I am the motherfucking boss."

"Say it back to me, Bombshell. Who's the motherfucking boss?"
-Guns

"You're suck a dick. You know that? But you're not defective. You're just... a special snowflake."
-Guns

"You're not the boss of my," she says in her sweet little princess voice. "My mom says I'm the boss of me."
-Guns

"I'm not sure I can kill Ford. He's weird. But I'm not gonna kill Ford. Or watch your back while you kill Ford. I might even like Ford. He's growing on me. I love Kate. And he loves Kate. So I'm gonna have to decline. If you try to kill Ford, I'm on Team Ford."
-Guns

"We like it like that, don't we? The dirty talk."
-Guns

"I want it here, Mr. Shrike. Outside, in the alley.
And I want it now."
-Guns

"I like you gagged, Bombshell. It's refreshing to make you be quiet. Don't get me wrong, I love your slutty mouth, especially when it seals around my cock, sucking me until I explode down your throat. But right now, I'm gonna talk business and you're gonna listen. You got it?"
-Guns

"Veronica Vaughn, why the fuck do you smell like Guns?"
-Guns

"Be my canvas, be my fantasy."
-Guns

"I love you Ron. It's always been you, baby."
-Guns

"I love you, Veronica. I love you more than I love myself. More than I love Ronin or Ford. More than the Team, Ronnie. I love you more than the Team."
-Guns

Spencer walked into my life, tipped me upside
down, and shook all the love right out of me.
-Guns

"Because, baby, I love you enough to push you away."
-Guns

"The first rule of Shrike Club is never to talk about Shrike Club."
-Guns

He's got so many names for me, but Ronnie-
that's the one that says I love you.
-Guns

Fuck me, she mouths silently. I lose control when she
does that and she knows it. Fuck me, fuck me,
fuck me. Over and over again.
-Guns

"Veronica Vaughn, this place will live on in our fantasies. You will remember this place for the rest of your life."
-Guns

_____

_____

_____

_____

_____

_____

_____

_____

_____

_____

_____

_____

_____

_____

_____

_____

_____

_____

_____

_____

LOSING
FRANCESCA

"I love you, too."

I refuse to hurt him, so if he tells me he loves me, I will say it back. And maybe I don't really love him like that right now, but I think he's right. I will probably learn to love him in that way over time.
-Losing Francesca

And I make a promise to myself to stay far
away from this boy. Far, far away.
-Losing Francesca

Fiona Sullivan is my soulmate. I knew it from the first
time we played together.
-Losing Francesca

I remember looking at her when she was four years
old and I was six, thinking to myself, I love that girl.
That is the girl I will marry.
-Losing Francesca

He kisses me again and this time it's very clear that
Brody Mason knows just what he's doing when it
comes to girls, because he kisses me thoroughly.
Like he's been waiting his whole life for my lips.
-Losing Francesca

"I want to, Fiona. I really, really do. But I told you,
when I kiss you it will be perfect."
-Losing Francesca

"And you will be the last girl I'll ever love like that. Ever."
Losing Francesca

"I mean, really. Pining over me since you were six,
it's just so damn sweet."
-Losing Francesca

"You're not about getting lucky, Fiona. I'm not even going
to kiss you tonight, let alone try for a home run."
-Losing Francesca

I've had to lose myself so many times, I'm not
even sure who I am right now.
-Losing Francesca

I relive that feeling over and over and it strikes me as funny that the feeling you get over a boy, the swooning, as they call it in stories, is real. I swooned.
-Losing Francesca

FOLLOW

Yes, my name is Grace Kinsella and I'm a filthy tweeter.

#GodIHopeHeLikesThatShit
-Follow

I am cheap. At least in this case. But I know better than to get involved in games. And I'm sure his game-playing skills are epic. So no. I can't sleep with him. At least not tonight.
-Follow

He could like choking or spanking or domination.
God, I hope he likes that shit.
-Follow

I'm not sure I could say not if he wants to have sex
with me tonight. And from what I've read about
him in the tabloids, he's dirty.
-Follow

"You're an asshole. God, I feel so stupid for having this major crush on you all these years. I'm so disappointed."
-Follow

When I look up at Vaughn, he's grinning like a boy
with a vibrator remote control in his pocket.
-Follow

I'm a talker. I'm a gabber. I'm what they call... social.
-Follow

Maybe all the women I date are toys, to some extent. But none of the women I date publicly get their asses spanked red or their hair pulled as I fuck them from behind.
-Follow

I crave the dirty, but only in private.
-Follow

"I can change, whatever it is. I can change."
-Follow

"It was nice fucking you. Good luck and goodbye."
-Follow

"I don't like you. It's that simple."
-Follow

He was every bit as much the Prince Charming in person as he is in the movies and magazines.
-Follow

I deserve more than to be a man's casual plaything.
I deserve more than to be a man's second thought. I
deserve the dream. The fairytale. I'm worth it.
-Follow

LIKE

And I have to admit, just the idea that Grace has been stalking me for so long, thinking about me as she's touched herself... well, it's more than a compliment. It's a turn on.

And maybe for the first time since I met him, he is speaking from his heart and not his dick.
-Like

"Listen, little blue bird, you're mine now. I own you, baby."
-Like

I'd like to fly to Denver right now and fuck that girl until
she relents and lets me boss her around.
-Like

"All that Twitter stuff. It's fake to you. Is that why you don't have a boyfriend? You prefer the illusion?"
-Like

Can I be your blue bird?
-Like

"Spread your legs, sweets."
-Like

One hundred and forty characters and a well
placed hash tag might just change my life.
-Like

BLOCK

Why can't I ever get what I want?

I give her everything she wants. I love her slowly. I
take my time and whisper in her ear.
-Block

You are the white daisy in that greenhouse. Your beauty is simple, your confidence strong, your feelings genuine.
-Block

My Prince Charming is out there somewhere,
his name just isn't Vaughn Asher.
-Block

"I might not be your prince, but I think you're my princess."
-Block

"Because you like me, Grace. You like me and I
like you. We're in like."
-Block

"We don't need the fairy tale when this is our reality."
-Block

You win. I'll be yours if you'll be mine.
-Block

"I'm scared. It's so much easier to want things
than it is to have things. Because having things
means you have to keep things."
-Block

"All your best intentions were nothing
but really good deceptions."
-Block

'You lie to yourself, I think. You're one long
string of self-serving lies."
-Block

'I'm dying for you, Vaughn. I hate you and I'm dying for you.
Why do you make me feel this way?"
-Block

"You can tell me, sweets. I can keep a secret too.
And I don't judge. I'm a good listener."
-Block

STATUS

"You're having social media withdrawal?"

"Oh, I forgot to tell you. This is a clothes-free zone.
You have to be naked. Sorry, that's just how it is."
-Status

'I don't just like you, Grace. I'm falling in love with you. I am, I can't help it. I'm falling in love with you and I need you to just stop blocking me and keep an open mind."
-Status

"Don't let me go."
-Status

God, this girl. She does it for me.
-Status

"Sweets, there is always time for pussy."
-Status

"I don't want to be your secret."
-Status

Vaughn Asher might not be a prince to the outside world, but in here, he's my hero.
-Status

"The princess always survives, and she does that all on
her own. Never mind the rescue - the real challenge
is surviving long enough for help to arrive.
-Status

'I love you Grace. I love you. I don't even care if that freaks you out or whatever. It's real. And I'm saying it."
-Status

PROFILE

I feel like I've been waiting my whole life for this girl. I feel like she is my soulmate.

"I love this girl. I'm going to marry her again and get her pregnant and spend the rest of my life bossing her ass around and pissing her off."
-Profile

I told her I'd never leave, and I meant it. I refuse to walk away, even if she wants me to.
-Profile

"Don't let the sad take over your life or make you afraid. Don't let it stop the words."
-Profile

There's no possible way I won't find you.
-Profile

"As long as I'm with you, I'm home."
-Profile

From now on, when life comes at us, we're gonna
fight it back together. We're gonna grab it by
the horns and ride the fuck out of it.
-Profile

"If you're sleeping with her, I will beat the
motherfucking shit out of you."
-Profile

"Please take me home, Asher."
-Profile

I'n not interested in dying to erase my pain
and I'm not interested in playing his game.
This time, he's going to play mine.
-Profile

HOME

"I'm in more than like with you, Grace. I'm in love. I'm so
fucking in love with you."

"I want you more than anything. I want to keep you forever and never let you go."
-Home

"I want you to spank me so I can cry. And then I
want you to fuck me and make it better.
-Home

"I owe you punishments, sweets. And I'm here to collect."
-Home

"I love all parts of you, Grace. There is nothing about you I'd change. I love all the parts."
-Home

"Be my prince and make me your princess and then I can deal with reality. But tonight, I just want the fairytale."
-Home

"I want to fucking devour you. I want to lick your pussy until you scream. I want to fuck your ass until you beg me to stop."
-Home

It says she trusts me. It says she loves me. It says she's ready.
She might not know it yet, but I do.
-Home

"I want to come down your throat, Grace. I want
to bury my whole dick in your throat."
-Home

"I love you. I married you. I want to fuck you and boss you around and make you have my babies. I want to keep you forever."
-Home

COME

~~ ~~ ~~ ~~ ~~ ~~

"You're mine now, Harp. You're mine now. No matter what happens, you're mine."

"That's a dirty little name for such a sweet little girl."
-Come

"Diving off a pier, to avoid telling me your name?
Now that... Harper, that shit is downright intriguing."
-Come

"Tell the fucking world you're down here with me,
lion fish. I could care less."
-Come

"I was really only looking to get laid tonight if you said yes and that was going to be the end of it. A few Coronas and some rolled tacos on the beach. Or if you're the fancy type, a seaside restaurant with an expensive bottle of wine to complement the surf and turf. The night ending with a nice hard and dirty fuck at your place so I can disappear in the middle of the night while you sleep peacefully, content with the multitude of orgasms I gifted you."

-Come

She is mine. She feels like mine.
-Come

"I'm not walking away from you. You need to understand that. Accept it. I'm here now and I feel like I'm doing the right thing for the first time in my life. I want you. I want to be inside of you. I've waited patiently for so fucking long. And this was a stroke of luck. Being sent here and finding you."
-Come

"You take away the dark emptiness, Harper.
You take away all the years of indifference."
-Come

"You can't see me. I'm invisible. You don't want
to know me. Because I'm no one. I'm zero."
-Come

I need a connection, even if it's based on
control and psychological manipulation.
-Come

Sex is power. I have some power over him. This man who kills people for a living can be at my mercy if I listen to what he likes and learn how to please him.
-Come

COME BACK

~~~ ~~~ ~~~ ~~~ ~~~ ~~~

"Suck it up, crybaby. I'm busy. If you can't manage on your
own, there's a school for Company orphans up in Montana.
I'll let them know you're coming."

Most of the time I'm OK with kids. I sorta like them. If I wasn't a killer, and my children wouldn't become property like I did, then yeah, I might have a kid.
-Come Back

Jesus Christ. You fucking girls. I've had it with
your emotional bullshit."
-Come Back

If death is a deal, then love is a promise.
-Come Back

"If I tell you to walk though fire, it's because I know beyond a doubt that you are fireproof. If I tell you to take a bullet, it's because I know that you are bulletproof. If I tell you to talk away from me, it's because *you know* I will come back for you. No matter what I tell you to do, you will do it, and you will be safe because I said so. Because I love you. Because you trust in my love."
-Come Back

"That feeling is James betraying you, Harper, And if I was you, I'd definitely listen to that one."
-Come Back

"I'm afraid to hope, James. I'm afraid to hope because
I think hope is a trap. Hope makes you want things
that won't come. Hope breaks your heart."
-Come Back

"I can't promise you we'll never be apart. It wouldn't be honest. But I can promise you one thing. If I leave you, I will come back."
-Come Back

How many dead bodies does it take for an
assassin to grow a conscience?
-Come Back

I'm so tired of being everyone's afterthought.
-Come Back

"I'm wondering how long I have to live. The last thing on my mind is the breakfast buffet at the Gold Strike."
-Come Back

I do know that trust can be easy if you want it to be.
You either do - or you don't. You believe in love and
 loyalty and good intentions - or you don't.
-Come Back

"You take away the dark emptiness, Harper. You take
away all the years of indifference and dissociation."
-Come Back

"This is more real than anything I've felt in years. Maybe ever."
-Come Back

"Jesus Christ, woman. You did not hear a word I said.
Just fucking trust me already."
-Come Back

Death is just a job.
-Come Back

"I trust you, Six. But you need to trust me too."
-Come Back

"I knew the very second I saw you. You were
my only reason to live."
-Come Back

"You can't have it both ways. Either you want
something convenient and fast filled with sex
and that's it. Or you want something meaningful
and you earn the trust that comes with it."
-Come Back

COMING
FOR YOU

~~~ ~~~ ~~~ ~~~ ~~~ ~~~

He kisses me and he tastes like freedom.

"I want to make you come, James."
-Coming for You

"Dude. Do not fuck with my Smurf."
-Coming for You

"I want to marry you. I want to take you away. Somewhere safe, and quiet. Somewhere we can get to know each other for real."
-Coming for You

He kisses me like he's the wind. Like he's the
sea. Like he's the desert.
-Coming for You

"You have always been mine, Harper Tate.
You have always been mine and I will
never let him have you."
-Coming for You

When the hunters show up, bad things happen.
-Coming for You

"Take it, Harper. Take all of it."
-Coming for You

I can't be your promise, it's wrong. But you're the
only girl I've ever wanted. I hope you know that.
-Coming for You

Eat your fucking dinner, and after we fuck, we can discuss.
-Coming for You

"Don't be too eager to get the happy ending,
Harper. Because getting there is the fun part."
-Coming for You

"If you die, James, I will die with you. Even if I
live, I will die with you."
-Coming for You

_____
_____
_____
_____
_____
_____
_____
_____
_____
_____
_____
_____
_____
_____
_____
_____
_____

Life with James is a full-color, full-speed ahead kind of love. I fell in love with that man. I did. I fell in love with the James everyone else hates.
-Coming for You

"We met years ago. We drifted apart to become these two people. And now we're back together. One soul, cut in half, reunited."
-Coming for You

"You have a number, Sasha. Not a name, a
number. You're Zero. The one no one expects.
The one who will set it all right."
-Coming for You

Grown men are terrified of him. Global organizations haven't been able to kill him. And yet when his cock is in my mouth, he gives me all the power.
-Coming for You

JUNCO

"You are the exhale after the kiss, Junco."
-Range

"I'd give up crying if I could just count
something besides heartbeats."
-Range

"I can't explain him, Lucan. He took me around
the world to kill people, for fuck's sake."
-Flight

"I'd rather float in the nothingness and drift away for eternity than get a stay of execution on my unhappy ending."
-The Magpie Bridge

"Men who want to kill their grandchildren
don't do those things, Junco."
-Flight

"Love is earned, not mandated. So I loved Tier back. Fiercely."
-Return

"You have very little faith in her, Raubtier.
I find it quite disturbing."
-The Magpie Bridge

I love this man so much but I can feel what's coming.
I can feel it. I push it down and snuggle up
against him, memorizing every second we've
spent out here in the little vacation house.
-Flight

She smells like the stars.
-Return

321

I don't want to take so much that there's nothing left. I don't want to use her up. I want to save her for later.

"Why would I be jealous? I can take you right here on the floor and he'd never know. Because you'd like it and you'd never tell him."
-321

"I'm in for the love, but not for the abuse."
-321

"No you dumb fuck. A sex tape, asshole. For fun."
-321

"I've never been so sure of something in all my life.
I want you both. I'll do anything to have you."
-321

"What needs to work? We have sex together, end of story."
-321

I don't know why I think that, I just know this girl
is the one. And if I have to play house with
JD for a little while to keep her. I will.
-321

"No, asshole. Because this week we're in a relationship."
-321

God I'd love for him to fuck me. Not with JD, but alone.
-321

"When? I'm fucking horny, man. And every time I touch her, she wants to come. But I don't want to start this shit off alone. You need to be there."
-321

"If you fuck her alone, I want it on camera.
So I can watch it later."
-321

"I'm only gonna say this one time, my friend. If you ever fuck her like she's a whore on the street again, I will kill you."
-321

"He will ruin everything. Because he cannot
have you. I saw you first."
-321

"I left because I love you."
-321

"You deserve the kind of love that has no conditions.
You deserve the kind of love that's free."
-321

ABOUT THE AUTHOR

JA Huss is the New York Times and USA Today bestselling author of more than twenty romances. She likes stories about family, loyalty, and extraordinary characters who struggle with basic human emotions while dealing with bigger than life problems. JA loves writing heroes who make you swoon, heroines who makes you jealous, and the perfect Happily Ever After ending.

You can chat with her on:
Facebook (www.facebook.com/AuthorJAHuss)
Twitter (@jahuss)
And her website: (www.jahuss.com)

If you're interested in getting your hands on an advanced release copy of her upcoming books, sneak peek teasers, or information on her upcoming personal appearances, you can join her newsletter list (http://eepurl.com/JVhAr) and get those details delivered right to your inbox.

41661608R00163

Made in the USA
Charleston, SC
04 May 2015